The P.O.W.E.R. of 5:

Reclaiming Your Power After COVID, Racial Injustice and Beyond

By Stephanie M. Jackson, M.A., M.Ed.

BK
ROYSTON
Publishing

BK Royston Publishing
P. O. Box 4321
Jeffersonville, IN 47131
502-802-5385
http://www.bkroystonpublishing.com
bkroystonpublishing@gmail.com

Reva and William Caldwell - Front cover picture
William Wiley - Back cover picture
Natural Multimedia - Cover Design

ISBN-13: 978-1-955063-46-3

Printed in the United States of America

Dedication

Thank you to my siblings for being my inspiration to BE the example. I dedicate this book to all of my family, students and families.

This book is also dedicated to **US** collectively reclaiming our power. For my people of hues of tan and brown beyond a regular box of crayons. The #POWERof5 is for those who still have breath in their bodies. Breonna Taylor, David McAtee, Travis Nagdy, George Floyd (and countless others who have lost their lives at the hands of others) including their loved ones trying to reclaim THEIR power. We will reclaim our power in your honor.

This is for those recovering from COVID-19, those who have lost someone due to COVID-19 complications and those trying to get back to a newer, stronger, more powerful way of living after the effects of living/thriving and surviving through two overlapping global pandemics in 2020/2021. This is for YOU for taking the time to reclaim your natural born POWER, by picking up your pieces. You are doing IT!

Acknowledgments

I would like to give honor to God, my angels, ancestors, my spirit guides, my tribe, all of my teachers, leaders, family, and friends who have been with me along the way.

This is for my grandparents: Charles E. Jackson, Sr., Emma Lee Jackson, John Kniffley, Sr. and Roberta Kniffley. My parents: Tammy Jackson Mason and Steven D. Kniffley, Sr. for giving me life and the sacrifices you made in my lifetime for me to have a strong foundation to be able to stand on, in honor of my ancestors and the human being God created me to become. To my Mommy, Valerie W. Kniffley, for taking me in as your own, your listening ear, prayers, and guidance. Thank you all for loving, guiding, and sifting me.

Bethany Kelley for your unconditional love and sistership for over 20 years filled with support, adventures, encouragement, guidance, and an example of the PHENOMENAL things one can do if we just give ourselves the **permission** to live life to the fullest.

Trinidad Jackson for your ENDLESS support, time, listening ear, teaching me, and selflessly learning and understanding the truth of who I am. You have been an example of DEDICATION and COMMITMENT in working toward one's goals. From you I have learned the true meaning of FRIENDSHIP and loyalty.

Thank you to my VILLAGE who've helped me HEAL myself along this journey of L.I.F.E. (Living in Forgiveness Every day). I appreciate you believing in me and the gifts that God placed within me to help give people H.O.P.E., Eternally. You've taught me, loved me, challenged me, been patient with me, gave me the bizness, cheered me on, humbled me, lifted me, prayed for/with me, and celebrated with me.

To YOU reading this piece of my heart. Thank you for taking the time to show up for yourself and being intrigued enough to go on this journey of reclaiming our power together. Thank you in advance for staying the course. The time is NOW! Let's GO!

Table of Contents

Introduction

What is power?

Power (n) 1): the ability to act or produce an effect, 2): possession of control, authority, or influence over others (Merriam-Webster Dictionary, 2021).

Have you ever felt powerless? What caused you to feel that way? What did you do to regain your power? Did you give up? Did/do you have the resources to help you regain your footing? If not, how did you manage? If you did, what helped you to manage?

We all have power. A power lies hidden deep within the core of ourselves, but some don't know, nor are they privy to the process of tapping into their power to cause a shift (change) in their lives. This meditation guide, journal, and restorative mindfulness practice is designed to help you do just that: cause a ripple of shifts in your life on a daily basis. I challenge you to stay the course, remain open to change, shifting and sifting. Allow yourself *accountable grace* by showing up for yourself (accountability) while making adjustments (grace) should you fall short. Fall madly in love with the person you are, while you are becoming the person you're destined to be. Yes, these shifts may feel uncomfortable, unrecognizable, and indescribable at times (like writing this book for example). There may also be times when it will feel so good to ya, that you giggle out of nowhere with unspeakable joy. Hahahahahhahaha! I just had to get that out because I feel it RIGHT NOW! A blissful feeling that I never want to end. It reminds me of the feeling Meg had at the end of Ava DuVernay's movie, "A Wrinkle in Time," an adaptation of Madeleine L'Engle's book. A feeling gently washed over her with complete satisfaction when she finally tessered. It's the alignment for me (being exactly where you are supposed to be at a particular moment)! The #POWERof5 is designed to assist you in taking back your time to create a shift, create space, empower, reset your mind, reclaim your power within, and ground yourself to prepare for what awaits you. Now, you may even use The P.O.W.E.R. of 5 to set the tone of your day in the most powerful way possible, any time you need to #POWERup your day between meetings or during transitions. Whenever you need it, it will be here for you. All it takes is five minutes. Actually, all it takes is the first second you take to begin The P.O.W.E.R. of 5. Let's go!!

How The P.O.W.E.R. of 5 Works

Simply put, take five minutes to show love for yourself WHENEVER you need it to reset your mind(set) and reclaim the P.O.W.E.R. that you possess in all situations. These five minutes are broken down into one minute of thought to (1) **P**ractice Gratitude, (2) have an **O**ptimistic Mindset, (3) create a **W**ise Plan, (4) **E**xercise (it's not what you think) and (5) **R**eflect on Your Greatness. After your five minutes of thought and consideration, how do you feel? Will you walk with a bold stride or will you shuffle your feet in defeat? The choice is yours. If it doesn't propel you to move confidently in the direction of your greatness don't give up, give it some time in different settings because it will take some time to retrain your brain with a new way of thinking. "We die to old ways of being to be reborn in our power." —Iyanla Vanzant's *Until Today Devotional* (2001, Touchstone).

When you feel powerless, BREATHE. Breathe for George Floyd. Breathe for Breonna Taylor. Breathe for Mike Brown, Tamir Rice, Sandra Bland, Trayvon Martin, Travis Nagdy, Tyler Gerth, and David McAtee. Breathe for those who cannot breathe anymore. Envisioning this should give you some perspective.

We must fill ourselves up so that we may have enough (as India Arie sings) "strength, courage and wisdom" in order to give of ourselves based on the gifts that we have within us to share. When we fill ourselves up, liberation is present and there is power in your liberation. How do you liberate yourself? I'll tell you! You live your L.I.F.E. (Live In Forgiveness Every day)! Telling your life story (or what I would call your "POWER Story") liberates you and sets you free from the bondage of thinking that no longer serves your greatest self. So let's reclaim **YOUR** POWER, together.

P — Practice Gratitude

It's April 12, 2020, and I don't want to get out of the bed, wash my face, brush my teeth, or even shower for that matter. I'm bound to these four walls because of this wretched virus (COVID-19) plaguing the human race. Wearing face masks is robbing me of the joy experienced when exchanging a smile of a stranger who passes by on my way into the grocery. I miss the warm embrace of my Granny, the love in her laugh and her words of wisdom. I began to think about wanting to go to visit her, but I knew I couldn't risk it because I love her too much and couldn't live with myself if I found out that she had contracted the virus from me, although I had been living in isolation for months.

Thinking back in this moment, in two days it will be the one-year anniversary of the murder of Breonna Taylor. I know I'm supposed to be talking about practicing gratitude, but just hear me out. I'm grateful for her life because she LIVED. I'm grateful because my community didn't allow her name to be forgotten. Activists like Rhonda Mathies, Keturah Herron, Hannah Drake, Kentucky State Representative Attica Scott, former Kentucky State Representative Charles Booker, Shameka Parrish-Wright, Trinidad Jackson, and young people like Travis Ngday (Rest In Peace), Nigel Blackburn, and Elijah Thomas took to the streets and their social media platforms to make some noise in pursuit of justice in Breonna Taylor's honor during a time when there was such a great risk (contracting COVID-19, casualties, and you name it). I am grateful to the creatives who used their passion, pain, trauma, and emotions to honor them in their work while cultivating their own healing and healing for our community. They were exercising their power. Their influence: their voice. I am grateful for their influence, their voice, their power. Let's practice some gratitude together!

~~~~~~

One-minute activity: Practice Gratitude

Set a timer for one minute to take some time to think about the things you truly have to be grateful for in this moment. What tangible or intangible things are you grateful for? The air you breathe, shelter, the ability to think, even the pain you may feel because you are alive to be able to FEEL. Write your responses below — LET'S GO!

_____

_____

_____

_____

_____

Reflective Action Questions:

How do your heart, mind, and body feel now that you've taken a moment to actually think about the things you have to be grateful for?

_____

_____

_____

_____

_____

How do you show gratitude for the things you are grateful for?

_____

_____

_____

_____

How can you show more gratitude for the people/things/experiences, etc., that you have in your life?

_____

_____

_____

_____

Based on your responses, what actions should you take to make the changes you desire in life?

_____

_____

_____

_____

O — Optimistic Mindset

"Optimism can save your life. Optimism is really good for your health. This goes back to how intertwined mental health and physical health are — making one better often improves the other." (Neil Peterson, www.ALLPsych.com)

How many times have you woke up on the "wrong side of the bed" only to have your day continue to get worse? Wardrobe malfunctions, forgot your lunch, someone cuts you off in traffic, you missed the bus, the presentation you were working on the night before didn't save your most recent brilliant tweaks to make your points POP! These are all just for starters. Have you lived in a space of "if it's going to happen to anyone, it will happen to me"?

Are you like me? Have you ever felt the overwhelming feelings of all that needs to be done when approaching a task or goal? Considering all that you've had to overcome just to be able to do the bare minimum. Have you ever struggled with thoughts that you don't have what it takes to get the job done? Well, I'm here to remind you that WE DO!

We deserve the best that life has to offer. We must believe and embody the feelings and mindset that WE are entitled to experience the power that our lives hold. The power is in forgiving ourselves for what we didn't, couldn't, wouldn't do before this moment. L.I.F.E. is all about living in forgiveness every day. In order to remain optimistic about life we must forgive ourselves daily for the ways in which we did not honor ourselves and the God within us. We must acknowledge, address, and forgive those for their wrong doings. If we do not, that lack of action in and of itself dishonors our highest selves.

Flashback to all of the times you gave up on yourself, your dreams, your desires. If you are a parent or a person of influence (EVERYONE), please keep in the forefront of your mind that you are your child's first teacher and you are teaching them (in action and deed) how to thrive in life (or not: no judgment, just loving accountability). The fact that you are reading this book shows that you are in alignment with your highest self. Whoot! Whoot!

There is power in your preference. Knowing what you desire is powerful because once you know, you can go about chasing after your desires with a laser focus. I affirm myself by saying "I'm FIRE when I'm focused!" It reminds me of my childhood years, playing video games when the character would glow or illuminate when it had reached a certain point in the game while collecting points. That is exactly where I want to be! Why don't you join me?!?

~~~~~~

One-minute activity: Optimistic Mindset

Just for a minute (set a timer), take 60 seconds to consider, recall, reflect, hope — DREAM, even! What do you hope will happen for you today? What do you hope will happen for you in your lifetime? What are your hopes, dreams, aspirations, greatest desires? Write your responses below.

_____

_____

_____

_____

_____

Reflective Action Questions:

What are you called/gifted to do?

_____

_____

_____

_____

What legacies (stories of you, pieces of you) are you leaving behind to make the world a better place? What's stopping you? Why? (**See the *Appendix* for more on legacy building**.)

_____

_____

_____

_____

What do you ALREADY have to give?

_____

_____

_____

_____

_____

What do you need to build a legacy/build onto your legacy?

_____

_____

_____

_____

_____

Draw pictures below that represent your hopes, dreams, aspirations and greatest desires. Feel free to be creative and outside the box!

W — Wise Plan

(Plan Your Work — Work Your Plan!)

Reflecting on your *optimistic mindset*, what action steps can you take in this moment or today to make your hopes your reality? I remember walking the halls of the School of Business on Kentucky State University's campus, seeing a little poster on the wall as you entered the main study room on the second floor reminding us: "Prior planning prevents poor performance." Sometimes it's easier said than done. However, if you put one foot in front of the other on a daily basis, your hopes and dreams can really become your reality. Take this book for example. The writing process has been teaching me that if you just do a little bit every day you won't be overwhelmed; greatness is manageable and attainable.

Creating a wise plan is the beginning of the process for cultivating a productive life. I even got stuck on this page for weeks while writing the book because I wasn't consistently planning my days. I get that this happens, but we owe it to ourselves to CONSISTENTLY show up for ourselves so that we are NOT burdened and overwhelmed. Tackling a little bit every day helps to stay above water so you can see more opportunities to show up and be present during this process of reclaiming your power. Acknowledging the actions you're taking daily (marking things off your to-do list) will help maintain an optimistic meditative state of mind. Meditation, simply put, is keeping something on your mind.

While creating your wise plan, it is important to plan to take time to meditate (intentionally think about something) on the greatness you deserve and are working to attain. While you meditate you can still think, receive knowledge from your highest power within you while you're driving, waiting, exercising, eating, walking, sitting, in transition, taking a bath/shower, getting ready for the day/bed, packing lunches for your children, cooking, washing clothes, cleaning…should I go on? Meditating on your *wise plan* and the great things you are planning helps you to see how you can maintain and manage it all. It also makes your hopes and dreams

9

more realistic while creating space for your hopes to become your reality. You must envision and feel it before it actually comes to fruition.

When we show up for ourselves we are showing up for others as well. How many times have you missed an appointment, meeting, opportunity, etc., because you didn't plan properly? Let's plan together, shall we?

~~~~~~

One-minute activity: Wise Plan

Just for a minute (set a timer), take 60 seconds to consider, recall, reflect, on your *optimistic mindset.* Based on your hopes, dreams and desires, what **three** action steps will you take today to create a *wise plan* so that you get closer to your hopes becoming your reality? Write your responses below.

_____

_____

_____

_____

_____

Reflective Action Questions

Do you use a planner? _____

If you don't use a planner, how do you keep up with your responsibilities and meetings?

_____

_____

If you do use a planner, what kind do you prefer (hourly, daily, weekly, monthly, or list your favorite combination)?

_____

_____

_____

_____

How do you plan for your day?

_____

_____

_____

_____

How do you plan for your week?

_____

_____

_____

_____

How do you plan for your month?

_____

_____

_____

_____

How do you plan for your year?

_____

_____

_____

_____

_____

Draw pictures below of you carrying out your "Wise Plan". What are you doing? Who are you with? How do you feel? How will you reward yourself? Feel free to be creative and outside the box!

E — Exercise

Question: When was the last time you exercised?

Yes, you read it correctly. EXERCISE! Before you EVEN go there, consider this: we exercise to strengthen our muscles. We have about 650 skeletal muscles to exercise our physical muscles. Yet, we must also exercise the muscles that are responsible for sharpening the skills, gifts, and talents we are blessed with in order to make the world a better place. What muscles do you need to exercise? Are there untapped talents and gifts inside you that the world needs to experience? Have you considered the skills you possess that would set you apart from others if you took a little time to take that course, do your own research, get that certification, or whatever the case may be for you? We owe it to ourselves to tap into the greatest version of ourselves for the benefit of ourselves and others. There is a level of KNOWINGNESS that comes from tapping into your highest selves that boosts our confidence and elongates our stride. We were all born for a reason and it is not just for ourselves or selfish ambitions, but to give to the world in intangible ways that outlive us so that it may be CHANGED.

We exercise to strengthen our muscles beyond the pain and to maintain a healthy lifestyle. It is important to press during exercise beyond the fear of the unknown so that we may live long enough to tell the story of our adventurous journey. Trust the process to be activated by a catalyst that will spark growth and change within yourself and around you. When you feel like letting up or giving up, take seven slow, DEEP breaths while repeating to yourself *"I'm FIRE when I'm focused!"*

If anyone has experienced surgery, an injury, physical therapy, or any type of therapy, we know that the at-home-work we are assigned are typically exercises to build our strength, reduce the scars and scar tissue related to our injury. The more we exercise using the tools and exercises provided, the stronger and wiser we become over time. Are you ready to get stronger? Let's GO!

~~~~~~

One-minute activity: Exercise

Choose one of the following exercises: (See appendix for more)

Choose one of the activities below, read it, then continue. Just for a minute (set a timer), take 60 seconds to complete one of the following exercises. Write your responses to your questions below. Remember to have an open mind if the activities are new to you.

- **Breathing Techniques** Slowly inhale and exhale for five counts each. How do you feel?

- **Listening** Close your eyes and listen. Put a finger up for each sound you hear during your 60 seconds? What did you hear? How do you feel after the activity?

- **Physical Movement** Choose an exercise or series of exercises to do: for example, jumping jacks, push-ups, lunges, stretches, sun salutations, jog in place. How do you feel afterward?

- **Visualization** Read over your response to the One-minute Optimistic Mindset or Wise Plan activity. Close your eyes and see yourself doing the things you wrote down. What do you see, hear, smell, taste, feel (physically and emotionally)?

- **Be present** Just sit and be present, noticing what comes to your mind. Write down your thoughts.

_____

_____

_____

_____

_____

<u>Reflective Action Questions</u>

What "muscles" do you need to exercise?

_____

_____

_____

_____

_____

Are there untapped talents and gifts inside you that the world needs to experience? If so, what are they?

_____

_____

_____

_____

_____

What tools do you have to help you exercise?

_____

_____

_____

_____

Do you have what you need to exercise?

_____

_____

_____

_____

What do you need to exercise?

_____

_____

_____

_____

Who can you reach out to for support?

_____

_____

_____

_____

How will you feel after you exercise your gifts?

_____

_____

_____

_____

Who will benefit from you exercising your gifts?

_____

_____

_____

_____

How do you think they will feel after experiencing your gifts?

_____

_____

_____

_____

How do you think those experiencing your gifts can/will make a difference in the world?

_____

_____

_____

_____

R — Reflect on Your Greatness

I Am

By Queen Savannah Sonshine

I-I-I-I- I am light.
Light that lights the pathway to the truth
and God within us all.

I-I-I-I- I am smiles.
Smiles that brighten up your day like a
beautiful sunset cascading across the
everlasting sea.

I-I-I-I- I am hugs.
Sweet hugs that engulf you like a tsunami
of love overtaking your...breath.

I-I-I-I- I am life.
Life, like the excitement at the beginning
of all of your hopes, dreams and desires
as they take flight.

I-I-I-I- I am hope.
Hope of my ancestors and my Father God
in my ability to stay focused and
connected to my divine source and
purpose for living.

I-I-I-I- I am queen
Queen Savannah Sonshine, BABY, sitting
tall on my throne built by my ancestors
gazing in awe of our inherited territory.

I-I-I-I- I am power.
Power necessary to obey my Heavenly
Father's guidance by taking up my cross
and living purposefully for him.

I-I-I-I- I am courage
Courage necessary to wait upon the Lord
in His timing to manifest miracles of
change within me.

I-I-I-I- I am wisdom
Wisdom from God to receive and hide His
word in my heart and apply it to
demonstrating my understanding.

I-I-I-I- I am peace.
Peace that goes beyond the
understanding of when and how my
purpose will be fulfilled in Him.

I-I-I-I- I am vibrations.
Vibrations greater than 432Hz manifesting
miracles, invoking healing powers,
emitting positive plush good vibes.

I-I-I-I- I am more
More than this pen can write, these
fingers can type, than your eyes can see.

I-I-I-I-I-AM-ME! I-AM-ME! I-AM-ME! I-AM-
ME!

I-I-I-I am...
Walking boldly in the knowingness of who
I am and who I am becoming.

I-I-I-I AM…

How often do you take the time to reflect on your greatness? The good within you? When was the last time you affirmed all of the pieces of you? Did you know that taking the time to acknowledge the pieces of you that you had to (re)discover that make you stronger, more confident, more resilient, and brave has sustaining powers? There are so many things that we encounter within a day's time that could potentially tear us down and steal our joy. It is our responsibility to keep ourselves lifted even if the world around us tries to keep us bound mentally, emotionally and/or physically.

God has placed gifts inside you that need to blossom and to bloom. You can facilitate that growth process by speaking affirmations about yourself based on WHO you are and WHOSE you are. There is so much rich goodness within us! If you are a parent, grandparent, god-parent, step-parent, aunt/uncle, or have children who are looking to you for guidance, remember that your life is the example of how they should live when you no longer walk this earth. Teach them by BEING the example of how to heal yourself and be fulfilled within yourself (themselves) by SEEING yourself (themselves) on a daily basis.

Only you know what life has been like for you during the times you are/have been stuck in your old ways because of past hurts (inflicted by self and others). I lovingly encourage you to do the work of healing your inner child/wounded self so that you can be FREE, NOW! Where can you start??? Consistently affirming yourself can help retrain your brain and heal at a cellular level (if you dare to believe).

Parents/guardians: you may not be able to financially give your child(ren) a better life than you had, but you can still GIFT them the PRESENT of a better quality of L.I.F.E. by living in forgiveness EVERY DAY. Forgiveness of self and others so that you don't have to carry the weight of your past hurts because you are FREEING yourself in each moment, even if you forget you can pick it back up while you retrain your brain to

19

remember a new pattern of thinking. I call it *accountable grace: holding yourself accountable for what you desire and loving yourself through the process when you don't always meet the mark you set for yourself and revising the mark.* Let's affirm our goodness together!

~~~~~~

One-minute activity: Reflect on Your Greatness

Just for a minute (set a timer), take 60 seconds to write down as you consider, recall, and reflect, on ALL that you are. What are your gifts, skills, talents? You are ALL of the "THINGS"! Turn them into affirmations. Example: *I am an artist. I am a good listener. I am a healer. I am a mechanic. I am a leader, etc.).* Write your responses below. *(Extension Activity found in the Appendix).*

_____

_____

_____

_____

_____

Reflective Action Questions:

How did it feel to affirm yourself?

_____

_____

_____

_____

What are the loving pieces of YOU that you'd like to rediscover?

_____

_____

_____

_____

_____

What positive traits and characteristics do you possess?

_____

_____

_____

_____

_____

What are your greatest accomplishments?

_____

_____

_____

_____

_____

When can you practice affirming who you are?

_____

_____

_____

_____

_____

What do you visualize about yourself while you say your affirmations aloud?

_____

_____

_____

_____

_____

Draw a picture, create a wordle or graffiti board of words that affirm who you are and desire to become. Feel free to be creative and outside the box!

Appendix

~~~~~~

One-minute activity: Exercise

Choose one of the activities below then respond Just for a minute (set a timer), take 60 seconds to complete one of the following exercises. Write your responses to your questions below. Gentle reminder: do your best to have an open mind if the activities are new to you.

- **Breathing Techniques:** Slowly Inhale and exhale for five counts each. How do you feel?

    - Alternate nostril breathing (Hold your right nostril down with your right or left thumb while slowly inhaling, completely filling your lungs with air. Then, switch and hold your left nostril down with your pinky finger as you slowly exhale. Repeat for 60 seconds).

    - Even-in, Even-Out (you choose the count)

    - Figure 8 (Take a nice slow inhale, then exhale your breath while making the number 8 in the air with your breath.)

- **Listening:** Close your eyes and listen. Put a finger up for each sound you hear. What did you hear? How do you feel after the activity?

- **Physical Movement:** Choose an exercise or series of exercises to do...for example: jumping jacks, push-ups, lunges, stretches, sun salutations, jog in place. How do you feel afterward?

- **Visualization:** Read over your response to the One-minute *Optimistic Mindset* or *Wise Plan* activity. Close your eyes and see yourself doing the things you wrote down. What do you see, hear, smell, taste, feel (physically and emotionally)?

- **Practice Being present:** Just sit and be present, noticing what comes to your mind. Write down your thoughts.

- **Repetitive Affirmation Journaling:** Write down a positive affirmation and continue to write it down for an entire minute. While you're writing, think of what the words mean to you and how you'll feel walking the words out in real life! Oh, don't forget to take mindful breaths between each affirmation.

- **Singing Freely:** Sing scales, part of your favorite song, or even make up a song!
- **Artistic Expression:** Recite a poem, draw, color, etc.
- **Gifted Reflection:** Reflect on how you can use your gifts today to exercise your power and influence.
- **Meditation:** Focus your attention on the thoughts that come to your mind and let your thoughts flow. You can also find guided meditations online or using a cell phone app such as Calm and Headspace.

~~~~~~

One-minute activity: Reflect on Your Greatness **(Extension)**

Just for a minute (set a timer), take 60 seconds to write down as you consider, recall, and reflect, on ALL that you are. What are your gifts, skills, talents? You are ALL of the "THINGS"! Turn them into affirmations. Example: *I am an artist. I am a good listener. I am a healer. I am a mechanic. I am a leader, etc.* Write your responses below. Find a mirror and repeat them to yourself while looking into the mirror. Take your time with it. Take a deep breath between each statement, REALLY feeling the meaning of the words you speak. Consider how hearing/saying these words makes you feel.

Document your findings below.

_____

_____

_____

_____

_____

_____

_____

_____

_____

_____

Draw a picture of yourself after you've finished the extended exercise. How do you feel? How will you show up differently in the world? How do you see yourself now?

The P.O.W.E.R. of 5 Legacy Building Podcast Interview Questions

Legacy Building —

How will/do you spend your time?

_____

_____

_____

_____

_____

How will/do you spend your money?

_____

_____

_____

_____

_____

How will/do you use your resources?

_____

_____

_____

_____

_____

How will/do you collaborate with your family or other families to build upon your family legacy?

_____

_____

_____

_____

How will/do you make the world a better place?

_____

_____

_____

_____

Draw a picture to represent your responses in this section. Feel free to create a picture that includes words like a graffiti board that embodies the legacy you desire to leave behind. BE CREATIVE!

The P.O.W.E.R. of 5 Journal Pages

Below you will find the guiding thoughts to complete the following daily journal pages. Consider purchasing The P.O.W.E.R. of 5 *Journal* to keep your journey consistent.

Practice Gratitude
Set a timer for one minute to take some time to think about the things you truly have to be grateful for in this moment. What tangible or intangible things are you grateful for? The air you breathe, shelter, the ability to think, even the pain you may feel because you are alive to be able to FEEL. LET'S GO!

Optimistic Mindset
Just for a minute (set a timer), take 60 seconds to consider, recall, reflect, hope — DREAM, even! What do you hope will happen for you today? What do you hope will happen for you in your lifetime? What are your hopes, dreams, aspirations, greatest desires?

Wise Plan
Just for a minute (set a timer), take 60 seconds to consider, recall, reflect, on your optimistic mindset. Based on your hopes, dreams, and desires, what three action steps will you take today to create a wise plan so that you get closer to your hopes becoming your reality?

Exercise
Choose one of the activities on page 23 or read it then continue. Just for a minute (set a timer), take 60 seconds to complete one of the following exercises. Write your responses to your questions below. Remember to have an open mind if the activities are new to you.

Reflect on Your Greatness
Just for a minute (set a timer), take 60 seconds to write down as you consider, recall, and reflect, on ALL that you are. What are your gifts, skills, talents? You are ALL of the "THINGS"! Turn them into affirmations. Example: I am an artist. I am a good listener. I am a healer. I am a mechanic. I am a leader, etc.

Date: _____

| How are you feeling/ what are you thinking before practicing The P.O.W.E.R. of 5? _____ _____ | How are you feeling/ what are you thinking after practicing The P.O.W.E.R. of 5? _____ |

P

I am grateful for..._____
_____
_____
_____

O

I hope this will happen..._____
_____
_____
_____

W

I will..._____
_____
_____
_____to make my hopes my reality.

E

Choose an activity and write about how you feel afterward.
_____
_____
_____
_____

R

I am..._____
_____
_____
_____

Date: _____

How are you feeling/ what are you thinking
before practicing The P.O.W.E.R. of 5? _____
_____

How are you feeling/ what are you thinking
after practicing The P.O.W.E.R. of 5?
_____

P

I am grateful for..._____
_____
_____
_____

O

I hope this will happen..._____
_____
_____
_____

W

I will..._____
_____
_____
_____to make my hopes my reality.

E

Choose an activity and write about how you feel afterward.
_____
_____
_____
_____

R

I am..._____
_____
_____
_____

Date: _____

| How are you feeling/ what are you thinking before practicing The P.O.W.E.R. of 5? _____ _____ | How are you feeling/ what are you thinking after practicing The P.O.W.E.R. of 5? _____ |

P

I am grateful for..._____
_____
_____
_____

O

I hope this will happen..._____
_____
_____
_____

W

I will..._____
_____
_____
_____to make my hopes my reality.

E

Choose an activity and write about how you feel afterward.
_____
_____
_____

R

I am..._____
_____
_____
_____

Date: _____

How are you feeling/ what are you thinking before practicing The P.O.W.E.R. of 5? _____
_____

How are you feeling/ what are you thinking after practicing The P.O.W.E.R. of 5?
_____

P

I am grateful for..._____
_____
_____
_____

O

I hope this will happen..._____
_____
_____
_____

W

I will..._____
_____
_____
_____to make my hopes my reality.

E

Choose an activity and write about how you feel afterward.
_____
_____
_____
_____

R

I am..._____
_____
_____
_____

Date: _____

| How are you feeling/ what are you thinking before practicing The P.O.W.E.R. of 5? _____ _____ | How are you feeling/ what are you thinking after practicing The P.O.W.E.R. of 5? _____ |

P

I am grateful for..._____
_____
_____
_____

O

I hope this will happen..._____
_____
_____
_____

W

I will..._____
_____
_____
_____to make my hopes my reality.

E

Choose an activity and write about how you feel afterward.
_____
_____
_____
_____

R

I am..._____
_____
_____
_____

Date: _____

| How are you feeling/ what are you thinking before practicing The P.O.W.E.R. of 5? _____ _____ | How are you feeling/ what are you thinking after practicing The P.O.W.E.R. of 5? _____ |

P

I am grateful for..._____
_____
_____
_____

O

I hope this will happen..._____
_____
_____
_____

W

I will..._____
_____
_____
_____to make my hopes my reality.

E

Choose an activity and write about how you feel afterward.
_____
_____
_____
_____

R

I am..._____
_____
_____
_____

Date: _____

| How are you feeling/ what are you thinking before practicing The P.O.W.E.R. of 5? _____ | How are you feeling/ what are you thinking after practicing The P.O.W.E.R. of 5? |

P

I am grateful for..._____
_____
_____
_____

O

I hope this will happen..._____
_____
_____
_____

W

I will..._____
_____
_____
_____to make my hopes my reality.

E

Choose an activity and write about how you feel afterward.
_____
_____
_____
_____

R

I am..._____
_____
_____
_____

Date: _____

| How are you feeling/ what are you thinking before practicing The P.O.W.E.R. of 5? _____ _____ | How are you feeling/ what are you thinking after practicing The P.O.W.E.R. of 5? _____ |

P

I am grateful for..._____
_____
_____
_____

O

I hope this will happen..._____
_____
_____
_____

W

I will..._____
_____
_____
_____to make my hopes my reality.

E

Choose an activity and write about how you feel afterward.
_____
_____
_____
_____

R

I am..._____
_____
_____

Date:_____

| How are you feeling/ what are you thinking before practicing The P.O.W.E.R. of 5? _____ _____ | How are you feeling/ what are you thinking after practicing The P.O.W.E.R. of 5? _____ |

P

I am grateful for..._____
_____
_____
_____

O

I hope this will happen..._____
_____
_____
_____

W

I will..._____
_____
_____
_____to make my hopes my reality.

E

Choose an activity and write about how you feel afterward.
_____
_____
_____
_____

R

I am..._____
_____
_____
_____

Date:_____

How are you feeling/ what are you thinking before practicing The P.O.W.E.R. of 5? _____
_____

How are you feeling/ what are you thinking after practicing The P.O.W.E.R. of 5?
_____

P

I am grateful for..._____
_____
_____
_____

O

I hope this will happen..._____
_____
_____
_____

W

I will..._____
_____
_____
_____
_____to make my hopes my reality.

E

Choose an activity and write about how you feel afterward.
_____
_____
_____
_____

R

I am..._____
_____
_____
_____

www.ingramcontent.com/pod-product-compliance
Lightning Source LLC
Chambersburg PA
CBHW081158090426
42736CB00017B/3380